Alpha Male

Develop Unshakeable Self-confidence

(Instantly Transform Yourself & Dominate the Dating Game)

Leonard Steele

Published By **Bengion Cosalas**

Leonard Steele

Alpha Male: Develop Unshakeable Self-confidence (Instantly Transform Yourself & Dominate the Dating Game)

ISBN   978-1-7776534-6-0

No part of this guidebook shall be reproduced in any form without permission in writing from the publisher except in the case of brief quotations embodied in critical articles or reviews.

Legal & Disclaimer

The information contained in this book is not designed to replace or take the place of any form of medicine or professional medical advice. The information in this book has been provided for educational & entertainment purposes only.

The information contained in this book has been compiled from sources deemed reliable, and it is accurate to the best of the Author's knowledge; however, the Author cannot guarantee its accuracy and validity and cannot be held liable for any errors or omissions. Changes are periodically made to this book. You must consult your doctor or get professional medical advice before using any of the suggested remedies, techniques, or information in this book.

Table Of Contents

Chapter 1: Understanding The Alpha Male Mindset

The most fundamental concept that is used that is essential to the understanding of evolutionary process of living organisms is "survival of the fittest." The idea is that, everything being equal, only those who are robust or fit enough to face the dangers and threats for their own survival get the chance to live longer and continue to breed with their kind. The fusion of nature's forces has no regard for those who are weak. This means that people who aren't able to protect themselves eventually risk disappearing.

The great thing about this idea is that it's not limited to studying of animals and plants. Actually, when we put it in the context of everyday life, it could provide a reason of how some people are successful in getting what they want, and the ways that others fall short. There is no place for dogs to play that exists, according to the popular saying, and only those made out of tougher material are likely to be successful.

The alpha male is here. In the past there has been a great deal written on what makes the man the alpha male. As much as research has been done on how to embody the traits that make up the characteristics, features, and other elements which make up the contemporary version of the masculine alpha.

But, what does one need to know in order to be considered to as an"alpha male?

On Top Of the Food Chain

The name implies that an alpha male one who is a symbol of standing at the top of in the hierarchy of food -someone who is a step above the rest with regard to physical appearance academic pursuits, professional endeavors, and romantic escapades as well as other aspects. It is the kind of person for whom everything appears effortless, and because of this, he is successful in all he does. It seems almost unjust.

Many of the qualities that help him stand out from all others define the male who is an alpha. With charisma, likable personality, a confident and steady manner of speaking with a clear and decisive appearance, as well as an unstoppable character, the alpha male is a man who knows exactly what he wants is totally passionate about the work you do, and is dedicated to achieving his objectives. This is why it's no surprise that those surrounding him can't be more supportive, but rather admire his achievements.

On the other hand, a person that is not an Alpha male can be described as beta male. Beta male is a demeaning term applied to an individual who doesn't has nor displays the characteristic characteristics of alpha males. In other words, a beta male is in essence an anonymous and unremarkable character who's life and career is characterized by insufficiency and a certain amount of routine as well as a deplorable absence of enthusiasm.

Lonely Connotation

In light of its somewhat lonely connotation It is not surprise that nobody wants to be referred to as beta male. This is exactly for men to adopt the mindset of an alpha male, in order to dispel any perception that they live in mediocre lifestyles.

They do not realize the reality the fact that becoming an Alpha male isn't simply something they are able to effortlessly attain overnight. It is actually a way of life or mindset which requires hard work dedication, discipline, and a consistent effort from you. Although it's the case that some of what makes you an alpha male can be genetic by nature, for instance the facial appearance as well as bone structure it is also true that being an Alpha male is an attribute that is able to be developed through time.

The following chapters go over in detail the various steps you can take to make yourself an alpha male for yourself. It is hoped that, while reading this guide, you'll learn the traits and skills that will boost confidence, develop a fun and attractive personality, display an enthralling attitude in the workplace and be successful when it comes to romance.

Chapter 2: Identifying Proven Methods To Boost Your Confidence

If there's anything that sets an alpha male apart in comparison to the other men this is that an alpha male acts and communicates with greater comfort and confidence than the men who are less confident. The way they conduct themselves is distinct from swag that is often a sign of the use of overcompensation in order to hide deep-buried fears or bravado. This is nothing more than a mindless excuse for being brave.

The term "confidence" refers to the ability you have to interact with people around you and perform things with no sign of discomfort, difficulty or apprehension. This is a crucial trait for establishing an authentic bond with people as well as performing your tasks smoothly and without any hiccups.

Though it's not tangible the concept of confidence will be evident to everyone who is able to feel or see it. In contrast, the absence of it can be just as evident, and that's the reason that if you strive to be an Alpha male, the only aspect you need to concentrate on is you can boost your confidence.

The quality of confidence is exhibited by displaying it in many different ways. From your manner of speaking and show your personality to other people It is essential to be consistent so that it appears you understand the way you're doing things and are at high-level of your situation. Being an Alpha male, you should never compromise your standards.

Talk Your Way

One of the easiest method for others to determine whether you're confident or not is through the manner in which you speak. The first impressions are the most important, therefore, appearing to be nervous and unfocused at the your first encounter is an issue that isn't easy to fix. Inability to address an impression of negativity will eventually lead to losing your reputation and may cause people to be reluctant to work with the situation.

There are a lot of options to use several ways to enhance your communication abilities. One of these strategies might not be evident, but it is being familiar with your target audience, or with the individuals you're talking to.

Knowing your audience will allow you to plan your strategy. It is due to the fact that a communication method that is effective for an audience that is a certain type might not work with some other group, creating a challenge when it comes to. If you do have an understanding of the people you'll be speaking to and what the age range is and what interests they have as well as what they work for and what they do for a living -- you are able to adjust and alter your method to find an approach that is suitable and efficient.

But knowing who you'll be speaking to is not the only stage. It is also important to enhance the ability to communicate with clarity and in a natural manner. The Alpha male is distinguished by their ability to communicate to their point clearly with the smallest amount of words. Do not create a habit of arguing the norm because doing this can only render you a fool which is obviously the last thing you'd want to do.

But, even though communicating with others should be an important aspect You should also be sure you are not perceived as a rigid or stiff person who is in that you are in business constantly time. So, make use of comedy to make your point. People love people who bring people joy or roar into laughter.

The laughter of laughter brings people closer. Therefore, the more relaxed the people feel around you, the more likely they will accept you as a friend. That is why being in a relaxed mood helps ease anxiety and allows you to make your case should you possess an agenda. It is then possible to leverage the other person's ability for listening to you to advantage. This is an important aspect of developing an appealing persona. This is something that will be discussed throughout the subsequent chapters.

Body Language

Beyond words, however the manner in which you speak and body language make a big difference in how well you're capable of communicating with other people in a confident manner. Communication is a process that encompasses an array of variables such as how you handle other handshakes when you give them an hugs, or the manner in which you stand or sit.

To begin, keep eyes on the people who you interact with. It shows that you're attentive to what people are saying and shows that you're paying attention. Take care, however, whenever you stare for in the direction of too much time, as people could be tempted to think that you're unsettling. Change your gaze from one eye to the next, or, when you're speaking to an audience of three or more people, glance at their foreheads or bridge between the eyebrows.

Take on the role of the alpha male through observing the correct posture. So, you should avoid slumping or having a slack manner of speaking. It's similar to the way primates beat their chests, and appear more taller for the sake to show their strength. If you're in your situation, however there is no need to engage in anything other than make sure that your general calm indicates that you're not an typical person.

To achieve this, you is advisable to greet visitors with a firm handshake it demonstrates confidence and determination. Also, avoid interacting of unneeded gestures. Be aware of yourself to identify if the gestures you use could be uninspiring or annoying. Then, make adjustments from there.

As a result, having confidence is something you should certainly work to improve as you attempt to develop into an alpha-male. It requires effort, determination, commitment, hard working, and consistency to ensure you can adopt the right behavior and do not appear like you're just performing for the sake of it.

Chapter 3: Sporting A Winsome Attitude At Work

One place in which you are able to display your masculine attitude is at work, and with good reason. First, you'd like to continue growing in the business you belong to. This aim requires you to be above the other employees to get promoted, or to have the chance to rise up in the ranks. A second reason is that being confident of your place in the workforce gives you confidence to be more effective. In the third, working alongside your colleagues is much simpler once they believe in the ability of you to perform.

Like everything else, the very first step you should take is be crystal clear on your goal and goals. There is no way to enter into battle without having an understanding of the cause you're fighting for, and in a variety of ways your day to work life is a war you need to win each and every time.

Establish your objectives and goals for the things you would like to achieve and the time frame to reach your targets. Being aware of what you'd like is sure to assist you to develop a career strategy.

After you've established your career path, you must get back to the essentials. It is important to concentrate on the main assignments and duties. It is simpler to take care of various tasks when you are able to master the fundamental tasks. This will not only allow you to become more productive and efficient, but also serve as an indication of your dependability and exceptional attitude to work -- qualities which will certainly work to your advantage in the course of time.

Assuming Your Position

Also, be prepared to be able to play your role. In your position as an alpha male it is important for everyone to be aware that you're certain about your abilities and secure about the fact you're an important asset for the company. The essence of this is that you are not flinching around your work and are in the know.

It will be beneficial to apply what you've learnt in the second chapter of the book on confidence and charisma. Be vocal and provide thoughtful advice but without being offensive or disapproving. Make a stand when you need to and do not engage in blame games. That means that you must take accountability for the results of your decisions. This means that you should take the responsibility to actively to shape your professional career. Doing nothing and waiting for amazing things to occur and not doing anything about it is a way to never even consider even a little.

Be aware, however, that when it comes down to taking care of your development in your workplace, having the status of an alpha male is the most dangerous of all. In the previous chapters, being likable and likable and having a powerful presence are a few of your most essential skills that you can accomplish to gain the appreciation and respect from your coworkers. But, it's not an exact principle. It is likely that, on some occasions, having any characteristics mentioned above can put yourself in a difficult position. How?

Management officials as well as human resource personnel could be worried that if you are always at the helm and always displaying an ebullient attitude and a confident attitude, you could feel the urge to do things independently and not be an effective team player. Be aware that in many, or even all, of the organizations that the capacity to display an attitude of cooperation and the capacity to gather the thoughts of the entire team is crucial. Also it is possible that you have the charisma and determination to get everyone to adhere to your rules however, if you're not willing to compromise and listen the opinions of others have to say, the possibility of being ostracized for promotion is a very real possibility.

Being Attuned To Your Environment

What do you have to accomplish to reduce this risk? Simple to be a good partner.

It's possible that you are asking: Aren't having an alpha male personality and an active team member opposites? Can these seeming opposite qualities be in harmony?

It is first important to be aware the fact that being an alpha male doesn't mean you ignore opinions of all the people present. Be aware that it requires maturity as well as class as well as a certain amount of sensitivity to take a moment and listen to what the others might have to say.

Conversationalists who are good listeners as well. The same way the best leaders are excellent listeners too. In all likelihood that the ability to listen is an essential skill the Alpha male must always have.

The key to the above is your desire to take in other people's comments about your performance. Be it from colleagues or superiors, receiving any type of feedback will always be an excellent way of determining your performance and to determine what else must be accomplished so that you can be more effective in the coming years.

Apart from keeping in touch with the opinions of others and opinions, it's equally vital to establish reasonable expectations of what other people have to offer. This is about perfection and its most evident negative consequences. It is important to note that men who are considered alphas are known for their strict expectations in their work however this differs from being the perfectionist. This refers to seeking to create the most of every situation and the latter, however, is a frenzied pursuit of unsustainable success which results in nothing more than dissatisfaction and unhappiness. Be aware of the differences.

To summarize, achieving success at work requires the right mix of insecurity and sensitivity -- qualities which alpha males are aware of. Being an alpha male you have a tenacious attitude in order to accomplish your goals, while remaining in tune with your surroundings. It is not wise to believe that if you just act in accordance with your instincts like an angry bull is enough to obtain the results you desire. A male who is alpha can clearly perform better than this.

Chapter 4: Ensuring Success In The Romance Department

One of the most interesting research conducted by biologists and specialists in the past few decades has to do with the dynamic of the relationships between males and females of particular primate species, like chimpanzees or gorillas. Researchers have observed that in terms of their sexual preferences for mating, females of these species usually prefer the strongest and most dominant male in the group.

There is there is a battle between the males in the group over who is the most powerful and hence the best suitable for the love of women. The battle is an intricate interaction of intimidation and even of physical violence that at the end of it all, results in the rise of an"alpha male. This Alpha male has the advantage not just of having the highest rank among the women of the group as well as becoming the group's official leader.

There is a lot of discussion about how the patterns that are evident in male and female interactions among primates can also be applied to human interactions. The theory is that women are naturally drawn to those who show the strength, confidence and the capability to stand out from other men. There is a consensus that this biological predisposition comes from within and is due to females' natural inclination to search for a partner capable enough to have children, sturdy enough to shield her from threats of any kind as well as a businessman enough to provide the needs of her children's needs.

Female Predisposition

In the case of human relations, the exact interactions that are observed in primates are just as apparent. Since the beginning of time many studies has been carried out in order to determine the pattern of human interactions beginning with how two people connect, form a bond and develop an alliance until those two decide to remain together and start an entire family with their own. It is a fact that women will naturally be drawn to men with an individuality and the ability to think for themselves, determination and strength characteristics that can be considered to be something other than mediocre.

If the female tendency to favor Alpha males over Beta males is innate and biological as a matter of nature should be investigated however the main conclusion from this research is that in the realm of romance, as in daily life, males who are alpha have an advantage that is significant over the majority of males. The way they make women feel attracted might seem to be an inequity to those who have worked all day long, yet do not earn the respect of women they cherish. But the great thing the good news can be that the status of an Alpha male isn't an exclusive attribute. It is something you too are able to attain when you put your brain and soul to the process.

The secret is understanding the internal functions of the female brain. It's naive think that women are automatically attracted to males just like they do. Contrary to the majority of men who's attraction to women is motivated by the short-term aim of capturing or subduing them women are thinking away from the immediate as well as into the distance. When they think about the future, think of their emotional investments, they imagine security, they imagine having children and then they imagine what the world will be as they age. In analyzing all these aspects, the logical conclusion is that people want an individual who is well-equipped to satisfy the needs of their desires, which is why they desire for alpha males.

In this way, males who are alpha enjoy a favorable situation where women view their ideal partner. This place demands that men who are considered alpha must be worthy of their rights, and in numerous ways, it's an issue that demands lots.

Based on the way they conduct themselves, however, it appears the alpha guys have all the romance stuff down already. They have made the whole appear so effortless. How do they accomplish it? Here are some methods they employ:

1. Learn the Art of Flirtation

This should be distinguished from loud, rowdy or even machismo-based attempts to get women's interest. It is important to know that males who are alpha do not belong to men who are the "Jersey Shore" kind of males whose concept of love involves drinking bongs, rap songs with explicit lyrics and uncommittal sexual activity. This is not the case.

The term "flirtation" refers to subtle actions that make women aware that a man is in love with her, but without necessarily saying the right words to express it. It could take shape in the form of genuine smiles, funny jokes and engaging conversation, in addition to other things. In essence, males who are alpha outline the way and then it flows smoothly to the end.

2. It's Not About It's All About

Yes, you've got the appearance, the wealth as well as the ability to command all the attention of everyone, but there is nothing that makes women feel more valued than being your focus. When you go out on dates, or occasions, you should not make the mistake of making it all about you. Also avoid talking too much about you or possibility of appearing as an insecure and smug child trapped inside an adult body in search of some kind of approval. For an alpha male one of the most important things you require is to be validated because, well why would you need it?

3. Make Her Feel Special

Give compliments generously However, you should be careful not to overdo the gesture. Be sure to engage her in a thoughtful dialogue about herself and her hobbies working, her most listened to music, as well as her dislikes. Be attentive and aware of how she moves and body language so that you are able to adapt to any rapid change in behavior.

4. Most Importantly, Be True To Yourself

To begin with it is not a need to behave in a manner that doesn't really represent who you truly have become. You've worked very hard to get where you are currently, so it's not a good idea to try to make up falsified claims. You're intelligent and eloquent. your appearance is impeccable and you stand out from others. The best thing you can do is take a moment to be yourself.

In love as well as the real world, males who are alpha are the most desirable of they. But, how can maintain your status as an alpha male over time? In the next chapter, we will discuss this issue.

Chapter 5: Imbibing The Alpha Male Persona As A Lifestyle Choice

In the preceding chapters, attaining Alpha male status requires an enormous amount of dedication and commitment. It may not be immediately apparent, especially when you consider how the alpha males appear to make things look effortless, but don't get taken in by their appearance. It required time and a great deal of experimentation and perseverance, determination and some degree of consistency in order to reap the results of their work.

It's important to note that being an Alpha male isn't a once-only practice. It means that regardless of what you've done to distinguished yourself from others There is there is always room for improvement and a chance to discover things that are different. Also, the habit of complacency is one which you must eliminate and eradicate in order to keep your status as a top male.

If you want to pursue a desire for personal development, you must strive to find a healthy and long-lasting balance between your inward and outward progress. In one sense, inside growth refers to your development of your abilities as well as your intellect and capacity. Outward growth, on the contrary aspect, relates to your physical health.

Never Enough

When it comes to growth that is inward involved, you should never become bored of studying. Be on the lookout for opportunities to enhance your capabilities and gain new knowledge to increase your understanding. The saying "Enough" says, never suffices.

Another way of enhancing your understanding is to look at those whose talents and accomplishments you admirate. Study their experiences. Find out what their top methods are, and incorporate these principles into your daily life. You can also try to do your own experiments and discover methods and methods that will assist you in improving your situation.

To grow outward The most important thing you can do in being an alpha male to be always in top form. In the midst of your duties and functions and the pressures placed upon you, it's essential to make an effort to stay healthy. Watch your diet. Also, at the same time you should workout regularly and spend the time to ensure that you appearance presentable throughout the day.

As a result it is true that being an alpha male can be both an aspiration and a way of life. Everybody wants to be an alpha however, being an alpha requires an adjustment in mindset and an effort to embrace different ways of working. Although becoming one takes perseverance and hard work and dedication, it's not past time to earn the status you've always wanted. Indeed, right now is a good time as ever to begin getting to the top on the food pyramid.

Chapter 6: Who Is An Alpha Male?

This is the sixth chapter in this book. Before we dive into the characteristics, features and ideals of an Alpha male, we should begin by understanding what is typically referred to as to be an alpha male. If you've watched films and read a few books, you would have a general idea of the model. But, there's more to the alpha male than muscular muscles that bulge and brawls with the pub.

A Roaring Personality

What would you consider to be an ideal personality? It is one that commands respect and is noticed when someone wearing it steps in the room, right? This is a bit of a lie. The personality is one of the most important aspects of an alpha male's profile. It is the aspect of you that gives initial impressions. I'll pause some time and talk to your about the first impressions. First impressions tend to be misguided however, they leave a lasting impression in the minds of those who are watching. Do not think about impressions. Often often, first impressions can do well for your. Clean-shaven, neatly put together in a suit, has better chance of getting the job than a poorly attired candidate who slouches in the interviewing room.

The males who are alpha have an attractive character. It is not easy for everyone to be capable of having a good personality, however it's not an impossible undertaking to create a persona. Do not believe that the appearance is the only thing that defines being a successful person. But they are not the only factor, however not as much that they are able to solely determine the course of your character. The essential elements of personality are explained in a few short points.

One of the most essential aspects of a great personality is their appearance. When we refer to "looks," we do not necessarily mean a good appearance. Good looks, however, isn't the same as the definition of the word. Naturally, your appearance matters and play a major role on how your character will be perceived.

Your body posture is a different aspect of your persona which you must take note of. A bad posture may cause a complete disorientation in likely situations. If you keep your posture correctly you are communicating a lot about your character since body posture is thought of as the body's language. It is possible to convey your message through your manner of speaking about, walk, or sit down and rise.

A well-rounded personality comes with beyond appearances and posture, proficient command of the art of communicating. First impressions are just so far. Then it's time to make things happen on your own hand, or to be exact. The language you speak should not just be correct but more than acceptable. If you are able to communicate yourself with accuracy, in regard to how you feel or think, you are showing clarity of thought. An Alpha male should be able to clearly think through a of what he desires or needs to say, do speak and think about.

Ways to Build A Good Personality

The best personality requires time to build. This isn't a quick procedure, but rather a long and more laborious process, or set of steps. To transform yourself into the most powerful Alpha male, you need to begin by focusing on changing your appearance from a 'also run' into one that is a winner. Sure, it isn't easy to do, but this the chapter will assist you to understand the various ways through which you could slow but steady progress toward the attractive personality you desire.

The first impression you make determines how much impact your impression leaves on the other side. Begin by thinking about what you can do to leave your first impression with a positive one.

Pick Clothes Wisely

Your first impression of you is determined by the clothes you put on. Since the beginning of time, humans have learned to cover himself with clothes patterns and trends, fashion updates are always in fashion. In the changing seasons, demands and fashions, fashion changed itself, and always has dominated our lives and times. The clothes you wear are an essential element of your character and shouldn't be overlooked in preparing yourself to stand out. If you look nice this shows you're an organized person who is concerned about the opinions of others about them. Beyond that it demonstrates you're a special person who can look after his body.

Learn about the appropriate occasion. It is true that not every piece of clothes you choose to wear will be appropriate to any of the professional or social events that you are an integral part of. This is due to the fact that there is an order to follow and an unspoken code of conduct about the occasion and appropriate attire you can wear for them. In the event of a violation, it could lead to a embarrassing social faux pas but devastating consequences on the impression that you make on people around you.

If, for instance, there is a gathering that is being hosted by your friends, it is possible to dress in shorts and a cute button-down t-shirt to suggest that you're attending some casual gathering. It's not just that a look fit the event however, it will demonstrate that you're aware of the purpose of the gathering and dressed to impress. It builds confidence with your friends.

If you are attending the office's celebration and you're a guest at the office, you could be a target for disciplinary action by wearing shorts, with a bandana and top with a hat from the beach. Naturally, you'd want to be expecting professional looks which would be dressed in formal clothes. Try to conform to the occasion prior to opening your closet this will lead us to our current topic for discussion that is the wardrobe.

Building Your Wardrobe

"Building your Wardrobe does not refer to the creation of a wood wardrobe using the finest timber crafted by a carpenter, and then auctioned off. The term refers to the contents of the closet. Your clothes must be carefully selected and arranged in a precise manner. The next section will provide the best way to start creating your personal wardrobe and keeping it.

Before we proceed I'd like to keep you in check and assure that it's an acceptable practice for alpha males having a dress. It is not the only thing that females possess in order to gain dominance. The alpha male's appearance isn't only about testosterone and muscle hormones. A male who is considered to be alpha is assessed by his clothes and also by his appearance.

Casual Occasion:

A wardrobe that is complete should include at the very least five shorts, pajamas, and casual pants useful in situations where you are just personal or family.

Official Occasions:

It is mandatory for your workplace to have formal celebrations that you're required to be a part of. Common sense tells us that you shouldn't wear casual clothing to these events. The best you can do is to have at minimum ten outfits of formal attire. Below is a guideline on how to choose the formal attire mentioned.

Pick a shade which isn't too vibrant and not too dull. Alpha males must pick a middle ground in choosing his outfit. The dull and boring color will always create a lasting impression for people who are attending an official event. Events that are arranged by companies typically are places where employees try to impress top managers and officials. If an alpha man is appropriately attired can influence to his advantage all possibilities of the scales.

Social Occasions:

Events for social gatherings can range that includes a neighbor's time in the gardens to gatherings of old friends. If you are looking to impress on these occasions, then look at the type of the occasion. Do you think it is inappropriate to dress casually for something formal? Is it too formal to dress casually? Make sure you dress according to your needs. So long as you aren't feeling unnatural and you don't feel uncomfortable, then you're ready to start.

Accessories!

If your wardrobe consisted of just clothing choices that would result in not be anything less than a fashion faux pas for you. Be sure to have items that can be stacked inside your wardrobe. You should create a space such as a drawer, to accommodate your items. Here's a short listing of common items and how to choose them:

Ties

The effect a good tie can have on the eyes of others is astounding. It may sound like a minor aspect of one's character however the actual game takes place between dots and stripes. Learn your tie-selection skills if are looking to impress.

The ties that have been striped look nice on basic in color and don't have a pattern or type. In the same way, dotted ties can wear well with dark-colored shirts. Be careful not to do it by mixing an untidy plaid shirt with tied in a stripe or with a pattern. The combination would be an absolute fashion faux pas. Plain shirts must be worn in conjunction with plain tie while patterns must be paired with attractive or pattern tie. Keep this in mind so that you don't feel uncomfortable when it comes to tie.

Wrist Watch

What's the point of your arm that you've built long and sweating weeks in the gym without the most elegant watch you can wear! Be sure to wear a watch at your fingertips, no matter what kind of circumstance that you find yourself within.

A wristwatch worn around your neck says a lot about your character. It demonstrates that you're one who is well-organized and will take your time seriously. It indicates that you aren't caught up in fancies that don't yield result or outcome. The wristwatch you wear on your left hand says more about you than all of your outfit does.

The dial of your watch can be bigger or smaller than the width of your arm. Most men, however, look more attractive when their dials are less than their arm's length. The reason for this is quite obvious the forearm needs to appear like one, and a dial can degrade the appearance of your forearm if it is dominant.

The metallic strap fell out of style in the past decade. In the absence of a properly-worn, metal strapped watch can be a big turn-off. Consider using metal straps in lieu of leather. Straps made of leather are not just more comfortable, but they also appear more elegant. Leather will always complement men's character.

Shoes

There are many women with a need for having their shoes in order. Shoes worn by men show his style and elegance. Shoes that are stylish could make or break your impression to those who are around you. Make sure you pick the right footwear for any occasion.

In the beginning, ensure that you clean any footwear you own. If your shoes look dirty, footwear can be as serious an irritant like potbelly. It is not a good idea for people to believe that you do not care about what you put in your shoes. Second, you should purchase the right tools to take care of your shoes. A flowering cherry and a toothbrush of appropriate size, and a cleaned cloth to clean difficult to reach areas will do well for a beginner. Finally, invest in an additional shoe rack in case you don't have. If you assign your footwear an individual space and you ensure you keep them neatly and you are able to choose your preferred option by walking through one of the doors.

Shoes in black are a timeless option. But, there are some instances wherein you are unable to have the money to buy black shoes. For a casual get-together with your group of friends or outing with colleagues doesn't necessitate wearing sneakers in black. To be prepared, that you keep on the shoe rack at least two casual shoes.

These casual shoes might be the slippers of a light or athletic shoes. Be aware of the event prior to deciding on your footwear.

Socks

Don't get assumption that something not obvious isn't. The socks you wear matter and not the same as other items, however they don't have a negligible importance as well. Incorrectly matched socks are not best for anyone who wants to become an apex male. There will always be a point on a daily basis when you have to take off the shoes and reveal the clothes you're wearing underneath your shoes.

Also, socks are important as they are the source of half of the smell you're expected to wear. The majority of men's smells originate through their feet. If you repeatedly wear your socks, this order, it gets more intense and may be a problem when it is not absorbed by your feet.

Nightwear

While technically, it is a fall into the category of clothing and accessories, due to its low use and the specificity of how they portray the wearer, I've made the decision to put nightwear under "accessories.".

Be aware of what you're wearing to sleep. Although there's no one to admire during this period, what you wear at night has a lasting impression on you. This ensures you're constantly aware of who you are and that no matter how tired or tired you've experienced throughout the day you've not neglected to care for your body. The clothes you put on before sleep is a reflection of the seriousness with which you treat your persona and what levels you're willing be willing to go to preserve the same. Also, being punctual with your evening attire shows that you have a specific style and behavior is ingrained into your brain's psyche and you can see it even in the day, when you're not tangled between your boxer shorts or undies.

In the event that you want to achieve"alpha" male label You should be able to choose from several options of nightwear. Boxers are an safe and smart choice because they're neither short or too big. They're a good size and have enough length to be subtle without looking as sexy. A similar alternative are pajamas. In certain regions, it's often referred to for its cardigan. Contrary to common belief the man wearing a pajama is more reliable than a man in uniforms. The pajama gives the appearance of domesticity and security. It suggests that the person wearing it is one who can be and rely on. The man would be concerned about loans for housing as well as life insurances. Not weekends parties or the alcohol brands involved. There's something sexually edgy about a pair of pajamas which can contribute to the points of alpha males scored by the person who is wearing the pajamas. The last but certainly not least be sure to not forget about the underwear you wear. What you wear under your pants can have the same impact on your appearance as what you put on over them. Choose brands that are well-known and respected in lieu of local-made underwear that may be poorly constructed and the threads of these products can cause issues such as rashes or other issues. Make sure you wear the correct size. If the package you are carrying is large and bulky, you should look for shirts which have more at the front. A smaller size will work with standard sizes of underwear.

Your clothes are your resumes. The clothes you wear is what you buy at the beginning. The impressions you make at the beginning stage can do wonders for your career. Be attentive to the clothes you wear because a man's reputation is most by the clothes he puts on than any other thing. The ability to maintain an outfit isn't just the exclusive responsibility of females. If you're in an habit of cleaning your clothes collection, you develop important habits, such as regularity, punctuality as well as discipline, qualities that are highly valued when it comes to an alpha male.

Physique

If there's one idea that pops into anyone's thoughts when the phrase "manliness" is mentioned and it's a body that has ripped arms and a toned body everywhere. Whatever your sexual preference an athletic body will always be appreciated by people at any level. This isn't just a requirement for health but has become increasingly a fashion that is to be followed. The better muscled an individual is and the more fit it is believed to be. A man who is an alpha must be aware of how well toned the body is throughout the day. To achieve this The following actions are recommended

Participate in the local gym and enjoy an individual trainer. Find a gym that is well-equipped within your vicinity and ask whether you can have personal trainers.

Because you are new to the game, you shouldn't overly focus on having an athletic physique and instead be focused on either increasing your the weight off or losing it depending on whether you're obese or not.

Check that your diet is in line with your fitness goals. Incorporate plenty of protein into your daily diet and limit your intake of hot and oily foods. Avoid eating out and taking food items from restaurants. It is essential to ensure you are eating in line with a healthy food plan. A healthy diet is having the proper amount of each item in the appropriate amount in your meals. The balanced diet is a source of the essential nutrients and minerals your body needs and provides it with all the nutrients it needs.

A fundamental requirement of the body you want to have is that it be properly fed and nourished at the beginning. There is no way to have an athletic body in the first day. It is important to be patient when building your body. This process requires time and the final body isn't going to be there in an instant.

Create a list with goals which you'd like be able to achieve prior to signing up for the gym's intense program. Do it each day, or week-by-week. Your goals should align with your capabilities and time. Avoid setting unattainable goals you set you in the gym.

Always strive to improve your outcomes and to have a toned body. You can only achieve this by continuously challenging yourself and pushing your limits that you'll be able to improve your performance. But, it is important to keep an eye out for overdoing the task. It is essential to build a physique in order to attain the alpha masculine status, but there's nothing more vital that your health.

Sort your training in gyms in specific areas and you'll realize the categorization of your workouts will work wonders for your body. Give each day of the week, specific parts of your body that you can work on. Begin by taking it one step at a time instead of trying to put the process.

Plan out the entire week. Try to incorporate your gym time into the schedule. Don't just grab your shorts to go for a workout when you have time. time to. Be sure to adhere to an exact schedule to go to the workout, to ensure that you can also master the art of discipline in the midst of your travels.

A well-tuned body is the desire of all guys and is a dream for each chick. In all likelihood, it's a fit and well-nourished body that draws women towards one another in a romantic way. The romantic quotient is not only improves the attractiveness for a male who is a macho, it can also increase his odds of having some fun.

Alpha males do not just build bodies. He cares for his body on a regular basis. It is possible that he doesn't attend a gym at an exact time every day, but he does take time time for a jog to push or pull up an activity that keeps him fit. He is sure that he's not just well-fit but also fit and healthy.

A muscular body is not just an eye-pleasing treat. One who takes the time to get a great body conveys a positive signal. Anyone who is spending time at the gym can be considered as a person who is patient and committed. If the shirt fits flawlessly in your arms it is evident that there's a increase in self-confidence, and you are no longer suffering with body problems. It indicates he is aware of how to care for the things he's given. This indicates that he's an individual who is driven to get things right and performs much work in order to accomplish the same. Anyone who exercises is someone you could most likely count on. He's the person helping you out in difficult circumstances. When you see a man build an athletic physique, he is a source of admiration and faith. If you want to be the next Alpha, you must get to the light of sleep put down the beanbag and begin working out. There is a chance that you won't end up looking good in one month, but you can hang here, you little rat. It is important to be noted that the muscled physique isn't all that the alpha male is. It is possible for him to be a rough-looking human being, yet still be considered to be the leader of the group. A good body can add a positive benefit for your profile as an Alpha male.

Chapter 7: Alpha Male And His Tongue

Hello to the seventh chapter in the book. While the title of this chapter may sound, I can assure you that it's not the way you imagine it might be. The chapter was created to take through an ideal male alpha and his speech patterns, that means he says that which he says.

In the last chapter, we discussed how an alpha male needs to pay attention to ensure his attire isn't just up-to-date but also suitable. We learned about the essential components of a great style for an alpha male. It was clear the importance of what you put on just as important as everything else. But, this chapter will be completely different from the preceding one. We will learn about the best manner of speaking that is typical of an alpha male. In the end, speaking what they are what they say.

If there's one weapon around the globe capable of outsmarting even nuclear missiles of Russia It's the power of words. Words are a source of energy that is inexhaustible to not just make amazing things, but also to demolish powerful empires. They are able to create or break your business. If you cut your words, it could cost you on a multimillion dollar deal. However you can get them correct and you'll be able to be the winner of the game. The power that words have can't be put into the words. They are able to alter the course of nations and determine the direction of history. Just like I stated at the beginning They are the most powerful weapon.

What is the significance of this chapter in the context that the novel was composed within? Men and words, they each do not make sense, are they? Let us discover.

The male who is the alpha in the group is easily discernible from a distance. There is no need to announce the arrival of their group as their mere presence will make it clear in a manner. Alpha males will never talk when it's not necessary to. The alpha male would always keep his mouth closed until the proper time to talk. When he speaks, the entire world is attentive.

Your character as the alpha male is determined by an array of variables. The appearance, the charisma, the body positions, and decision-making abilities and the list continues much longer and more than even the Great Wall of China. One of the most important aspects that people often miss in the process of determining methods to build an elite male character is the ability to speak.

What You Speak

A male who is an alpha will never mince his phrases. He is aware of the precise meaning of the words he speaks. He's more aware than to just go through the verge of a verbal diarrhoea, and then swing the words around. He's an experienced speaker, someone who is aware of the ingredients he uses and their benefits, as well as the flaws as well as possible ideas.

A male who is an alpha does not come up with terms on the spot neither does he think about' something until the appropriate time comes. In terms of speaking the alpha male usually prepared, or arrives equipped with a complete set of homework. If you wish to become the alpha male of your generation, you should first master the skills of research. Imagine speaking to people for to convince the audience of your ideas. Do you just randomly go on stage pick up the mic and blabber on about whatever you can think of? If you do, would you rather go back to the house, research and make a note of points that you'll be addressing, then return and begin dressing the crowd with respect? As an alpha male seeking position, you'll opt for this option, and it is as a speech which is poorly prepared and not thoroughly research will certainly affect the impression of your audience.

The words you speak can be a significant factor in making your decision about the status of an alpha man. Alpha males only say the things which are needed without fuss. Alpha males are eloquent and can distinguish his "their" from his 'there'. He is able to be concise, instructive and still welcoming.

How You Speak

Of course, the most important aspect of speech is how you talk, the tone of your speech is much more crucial than the content. The way you talk is more important than what you're saying.

The ideal Alpha male has the right way to communicate in circumstances that require a particular manner of speaking. He can address groups, crowds, and mass. He can speak to the help-seeker. He is familiar with the words of comfort to a grieving person. He knows the tones one has to perform based on the various conditions. The moods, as well as their tones are stored in the mind of an alpha male's database and can be controlled by to modify them as he pleases.

Gentle

A gentle male can be found with his words in specific situations. These situations might involve an individual seeking assistance or an afflicted member of the group who needs advice or comfort. The alpha male is believed to serve as the father figure in the group, and a character should show compassion and loving. Care and love is shown through use of appropriate phrases, but more frequently than not, it's the kind words that can do what they are supposed to do.

Soft

The distinction between being soft and gentle is the fact that when being gentle, you are doing at a higher level in regards to your behavior, whereas when you're being soft it is in regards to the volume and tone. A male who is alpha isn't only gentle, but also a soft. It is important to not just limit the volume of your speech but how often you use it.

Firm

The fact that an alpha male is expected to be popular and therefore should have a soft and gentle speech, it doesn't mean that he can't be a firm person like three of the above. The art of being firm in your speech is about honesty, being straight and consistent in your speech.

Speech firmness does not have to be emphasized or shown in a separate manner. Your way of speaking indicates that you're firmly to your convictions and conducted enough research so that you don't change your mind about them. The decision is yours, and nobody is anyone else's.

When You Speak

The alpha male not only knows the best ways to communicate but he also knows when to talk. There's the time for everything in the world. Wall clocks do not display an accurate time. It is best to determine it using your the experience of others and your own. Alpha males do not get started on a rant the very first chance he has at putting his opinions on others' faces.

A male who is an alpha knows when to put his head down and when to share his views. When you express an opinion, the timing is just as crucial as the substance. It is possible that you have a hefty vocabulary and an old-fashioned baritone to brag about however, if you're someone who is unable to form an clue about how to use his mouth and how to close the door, you're just the same as a muffled.

Your timing for speaking should not be only precise, but also appropriate. You must recognize when your viewpoint is necessary and when it's not. It is not enough to keep track of such occasions however, you must also keep note of when these situations occur. There's always an underlying pattern that emerges within a discussion, and this could help you identify exactly the time that your opinion will have significance to the audience. Only that you can begin to understand how to calculate or anticipate these instances that you grow as a presenter. There are instances when no anyone wants your opinions. In other instances, there is no need for your opinion however it is vital for your own good to make it known before everyone, regardless of whether they want that or not. There are also times when everyone demands you to be heard. Make sure you are able to assess the circumstance and categorizing it according to the categories. Be alert to opportunities when you see someone making a mistake. Take advantage of the chance with both hands and then speak. There's nothing such as the ideal time to talk. As was mentioned in the beginning of this chapter clock on the planet is programmed to give you the right time for speaking. It's only through practice during group meetings as well as a bit of general sense that you'll be able to estimate the time to speak.

No Bullshit Attitude

Alpha males never beat at the drum. If he is asked to talk about the subject, he will swiftly cut right to the chase and make only the point which he believes are relevant to the audience, topic of that are being discussed as well as time constraints. You should not spend your time by analyzing the background of the issue, or its potential influence in the near future, or what expectations the public may hold about the topic. The expert will give you the hard-hitting factual information that has been proved and can help you to save your time.

Did you participate or attend in debates while you were in high school? Perhaps you wrote an essay on the environment and peace around the world in the eighth grade? If you answered yes, then you be aware of what I intend to discuss. The act of speaking in bullshit is one which is used in order to avoid the primary point entirely avoided, but also to divert the conversation in an unrelated direction in relation to the point of the conversation.

If an alpha male is speaking the people pay attention. He is distinctive from the other men because he's clear and appears to be honest. If you'd like to be the alpha male of your speech, master the art of cutting all unnecessary things includes everything that is valuable and pertinent. Be able to discern between the common and the vital. You can tell from male who is an alpha is an individual with the knowledge, expertise and experience on whatever topic he's speaking about. He is not somebody who's just winging it on the fly or speaking from his backside.

Speaking is crucial to the formation the alpha male position. Alpha males know the right way, what to say, and in what amount to talk. He never stray from the truth and is committed to staying true to the essence and as truthful as it is. He's charming, soft well-mannered and polite. He is also incredibly talented when it comes to vocabulary. His vocabulary is elegant, straightforward and wealthy. He can keep an audience engaged without taking them away from the subject that is being discussed for one second. His audience doesn't get disinterested for the slightest fraction of a second. It can comprehend what he says. A true alpha male is able to attract his followers. He makes use of the most basic words to guide you through the tale. Alpha males are an excellent storytelling expert. He'd gather his personal memories into a tin and then pull them each one out depending on the circumstance and the context. He is a teller of tales to relate. The audience isn't just impressed by him, but they also admire his public speaking ability.

A male who is alpha is the perfect speaker. He is aware of everything to learn about public speaking. He understands how important it is to know the precise time to stop, take for a moment, or even occasionally sigh. There are always examples of a perfect alpha male speaking to an audience at an event, inspiring a group of children at a rally, or organizing a demonstration against a blatantly unjustified government ban. There are plenty of examples of men who have the status of speaking well are plentiful all over the world. It is important to recognize that the opposite cannot be to be the case. Some good speakers are not specifically suited to be Alpha males. They may possess the gift of speaking, but in satisfying the other demands of an ideal Alpha male they are not meeting the requirements of the requirements that are asked for. The art of communication is just one element of the ideal alpha male character. It is a part that adds charisma of an alpha male, but it is not the entire package. However, it's an important feather that needs to have in your cape.

Alpha males have the ability to accomplish impossible feats using only words. He is able to get maximum results from using the correct words. To achieve this it is necessary to first possess the ability to comprehend a wide range of words. If you want to develop your vocabulary, begin by reading your newspaper in the morning. Learn the meanings of those words that you didn't comprehend by looking up the Internet or using a dictionary. Nowadays, they're permitting you to download offline dictionary to your phones. A well-known vocabulary is always a good thing and earns your brownie points. A male who is an alpha makes the best usage of an extensive vocabulary in order to make positive impressions. A male who is alpha knows the correct word choice depending on the specific circumstance.

It is rare to see an Alpha male who is fumbling around with his word choices. He is a man who takes his time and pauses between while pondering words, and releases them with a professional manner. His style, tone and delivery are suitable for the setting that he's in. Therefore, it goes without the fact that an Alpha male has a superb presenter. The charismatic speaker can retain an audience for long hours.

There is a lot you can learn about someone based on the manner in which they talk. Your words eventually become the persona you are. An excellent example is the inspirational words left to us by great individuals. Take a glance at the brilliance of some truly inspiring quotations from Mahatma Gandhi, Plato along with other famous people and it is easy to define their personality. The same way that, an alpha male will be assessed by the way he speaks and how he talks. Every word coming from his mouth is evaluated and measured. If you're looking to become the alpha male of your generation and have been working on your speaking skills Here is a short checklist of tips to help your. Focus on the words that are important and cut out the unnecessary parts. Reduce the amount of words you speak in the allotted time. Don't take up excessive time of the audience. Keep to the format you have established and avoid boring your audience with facts or numbers. You can include stories and humorous examples for some humour. Keep the eye contact of your viewers. The more eye contact that you have made your audience, the more authentic you appear as an actor. Making mistakes is fine; just remember this; however, correcting your mistakes is crucial. Do your practice before the mirror one hour prior to the time you're about giving your speech. The risk of fumbling can be held at bay by doing this. A second thing that should being kept in mind is to increase your vocabulary every time feasible. A well-developed vocabulary is an attractive thing that you can be proud of, and it's never a bad idea to use good language when using them.

Chapter 8: Basic Features Of An Alpha Male That You Must Incorporate Into Your Personality

Hello to the eight chapter of the e-book. The chapter is made to inform you of the fundamental characteristics of an alpha man that should be integrated in your daily life so that you can to take a step further toward becoming an alpha male. Be aware that this book doesn't guarantee you a quick change into a jolly massive mass of masculine power, however it will provide you with the steps. It is time that we made the leap without any fuss.

In the next paragraphs, you will discover the fundamental characteristics of a typical Alpha male to help you on your way to supreme masculinity.

Responsible

Alpha males are someone who is responsible. He is aware of what's required of him and goes through his tasks in a manner that is appropriate. Responsibility is rare that cannot appear in the herd of people.

The main difference between the common folks and alpha males is that alpha male does not suffer by expectations. They are individuals who are a part of the group and don't consider them to be the sole responsible party for any major incident that happens to the entire group. The second group of people, known as the Alpha males on the other side, are mature individuals that are well-aware of their duties and behave accordingly. The alpha male will always be aware of his obligations and make them the top priority. The alpha male would seek out methods to resolve issues that result from his having difficulty fulfilling the obligations he has. He should be ready to deal with the worst-case scenario and perform mental exercises of everything possible outcomes if something did not go as planned.

The leaders of the group are able to be expected to assume the responsibilities just like a real man. This expectation was all through the history of humanity. Prehistoric times each tribe had the leader, who took crucial decisions and distribute instructions. In the modern world, and you'll find an individual leader as well as team leaders in each corporate established. They are all an alpha male in their own ways because they have the responsibility of their whole group. If the team is afflicted with loss, it's going to be their fault and they will bear the responsibility. If a team performs without a hitch the majority of the awe is bound to be reserved for the team.

A Complete Leader

Alpha males are an ideal leader. Every team has the leader, the captain along with a monitor, and finally a supervisor. The term leader can be used to refer to different times, places and circumstances. Whatever way you spell it or refer to it, the person who is accountable for the performance of the group and who is in charge of the entire group and every member of it, is considered to be a leader in the entire group.

Leader vs. Boss

A male who is an alpha in order to be one is the leader. The term "leadership" isn't synonymous with managing, though. What distinguishes the two is the difference between a boss and a leader. A boss will have people work under his direction, while the leader will walk down his high stairwell and collaborate with his team. The leader is a person's one and is not merely an obese king sitting on at his throne or directing the castle. The leader is aware of his employees as well as their strengths and weaknesses.

Alpha males not only is aware of his group, but engages them regularly. He knows the characteristics of his group's members. He is the sole person within the group that can determine the best method to utilize these qualities to serve the good of the group. They are similar to sleeping volcanoes. They can never get activated unless they are pushed to act. The leader is aware of the potential of each one and pushes them in their best form. Leaders are aware of the limitations and speed that the group's members, and knows the proper amount of energy needed to bring these traits into action.

What differentiates the two is the distinction between Hitler as well as Gandhi. Both headed a nation. However, when Hitler was a leader from the top of his horses, Gandhi decided to work alongside his followers instead of being in comfort or shouting commands from the seat on the throne.

A male who is alpha isn't an employee, but rather an effective leader. He is aware of his group inside and out. He is aware of the limit that his team can go to. He knows his individual abilities and knows how every member is allowed to play a specific job. When a person is suffering from trouble, he is able to talk about it with the leader, just like you would if he were nothing other than a acquaintance. A leader's impression on the group members is warm and cosy. The leader isn't someone who everyone is afraid of, but is a person that everyone admires. Being a leader equates with being able to create admiration and respect. It doesn't have to be declared that the leader has entered the room. Once a leader walks into the room, all are instantly conscious of his presence because of the way he walk. The leader is the only one present in the room that is not required to introduce himself in any way. He knows everyone in his team and has contact with them personally.

An excellent leader will push you to the limit. Yet, your boss does not take note of the capabilities you have. The boss might not have a clue about your own capabilities and abilities. But, if you're in the hands of a boss and he knows the things you are able to do and not be able to do. Leaders bring your best by pushing you until your limits. He's ready to push you back when you begin breaking, but when you don't the right thing, he will not hesitate in making you vulnerable to your biggest fears. He'll encourage you to smash all of your records in the past. He will not let you relax until you've finished the race. He'll shout at you, scream at you, and even encourage the moment you fall off however he will not let you down. Someone like that is there for you regardless of the situation. He'll become your dad figure through the thick and thin. However much you fail in your game the man will stand by your aid and support your hand. He won't fight your battles, but push you to take action without a helper. This kind of man is the best man to be around in your life, as you'll have constant assistance and guidance.

The personality of an alpha male isn't that different when compared to a leader's. The characteristics that define leaders and of an alpha male don't seem to be very distinct from one another. If you take a close look it will become apparent that an individual who's naturally a leader will most likely become a man that is likely to becoming an Alpha male.

The Decision MakingGroup whichever it might be, whatever end-point the group is in pursuit of and whatever the charismatic leader it is with, if decision-making processes within the team are not logical and unproductive, it is a sign that something is wrong with the male who is the top leader of the team.

The ability to distinguish the right from the wrong or left from right, black from white and all that among other things is a rare ability. Most people can't discern between these simple aspects within their daily lives, which are in addition to the shock and awe, strikingly different from the other. The capacity to think and make a choice is a crucial quality that must be found at a high level in everyone that has earned the status of being an Alpha male.

Alpha males, like the one we saw a few pages ago is an honest man. His shoulders carry all of the look-seeing glasses that define victories and losses. He is accountable for all that the team through, does and doesn't succeed to achieve in. When this happens it is essential for the male who is considered to be the top leader to make every decision using a sense of sagacity, wit and discretion.

Prudence refers to the quality of someone who remains rational in the way he approaches everything in his the world. Also, it could be stated that the trait of prudence is a crucial element of the alpha male character. Prudent people are sensible person who makes decisions from the classic logical perspective.

The ingredient of wisdom is the main one of the dish "decision". The ability to gain wisdom is not acquired over night. There is no book that can help you attain wisdom, unless you've been through enough suffering to understand the value of it. It isn't knowledge. It is what you know but wisdom is the realization of the fact that you do not. There is a need for information, but you'll not ever thirst for knowledge. Knowledge humbles you, and wisdom can make you feel very proud. The ability to gain knowledge can be obtained by reading books or reading scripts, however wisdom can only be gained from years of experience as well as plenty of common wisdom. A man who is alpha can be intelligent and can make informed choices.

It's not always easy to remain calm when there's chaos in the surrounding area. Imagine having to make an important decision in such an time in danger. It is not just possible to make the wrong decision however, you're also likely to make a decision which could backfire against the entire group. A male who is alpha has the capability of retaining his in the right place while making tough decisions.

The choices are difficult especially when you are making them for other people. Alpha males do precisely that. He's responsible for everything that happens to the team when that he hits on the Enter button. This is why it's crucial for an alpha male to make sound decisions at the right time.

Recognizes Potential

A group, or a team does not just revolve around its leader. The members of a group are as valuable in the same way as their leader. In spite of the position of being an important administrative position and the position of leader, the leader is able to speak on critical or vital issues while not reducing the importance for the other group members.

Everyone in the group can be tapped into a certain potential to be utilized to benefit the whole group toward achieving a objective. Alpha males know how to best tap into the potential in a person and the best way to utilize to achieve the stated goal. A male who is an alpha spends a significant amounts of time in his home, asking questions about his staff and staying up-to-date on each person's health. If he engages in such an activity, he comes to learn a lot of things. From these aspects, among the most significant aspects are: a person's capabilities, limits in their behavior, fears and areas of improvements. He draws a mental picture of everyone who he spoke to, met and observed in his travels and then invites those who are on the map. The alpha male is now able with the ability to reach anyone and test and test their skills. When this evaluation stage has been completed, the Alpha male assigns to each of the members his work that he believes is suitable for them based on the conclusions derived from his evaluation.

A leader who is an alpha must keep an eye out for potential talent and adept skills. A keen eye on potential candidates is beneficial not just the leader but the entire team. With his team members well-known inside out, he's at the ideal place to allocate the work and to expect outcomes.

Accountability

Alpha males are an individual who is entrusted with responsibility. Two scenarios are that the alpha male is held accountable for his actions for the outcome of the team's the desired result and also when they suffer losing. In both instances, the male who is alpha accountable for the results. Since he is the caption of the group, it's the duty of the captain to ensure that any decision is taken is in the best team's interests and helps propel it to winning.

The best kind of alpha males is different with regard to accountability. The breed is adamant and accepts the full accountability when the team is underperforming or falls short. The individual goes into defensive mode, and is trying to minimise the effects of the defeat. When the team is successful an Alpha male step down and let the whole team be the ones to take the credit which reduces the importance of his contribution to winning, however big it might have been. A true alpha male strives about accountability, however once the accolades are flooding in, He folds his hands in a fist and stands at the corner, so that he can let his team bask in the satisfaction.

Charismatic

Although it isn't the most stringent of standards, a likable leader that aspires to be the leader of the group is a great choice. When you've put the effort to become the most masculine member of your team, if you can sprinkle some glamour on top and the food becomes irresistible.

Nobody can not be able to resist the charisma that is poured out by a person who is a leader, responsible and the one who makes decisions. If you're charismatic, people will not only look up at you but also at your. Charisma when you are a possible alpha male can be an attractor of attention and can certainly turn the women to your direction. It may seem a little tinny to draw attention through looking however, you have to take the steps you need to accomplish. Charisma gives you that first boost that many leaders do not have. If you're charismatic, you are inevitably the most talked-about talk of the town and more popular than those who come in with a slack charismatic button. Charisma isn't something to boast about; nevertheless, it may tip the odds in your favor. Charisma does not mean beautiful looks, however. It is possible to be charming even if you're not beautiful. The issue is what you appear more than what you appear to be. It's also about the way in which you portray your self-image, no matter the clothes you wear or how you appear. Hit that charisma button and let out the masculine side of yourself.

Creative

Alpha males are not just about muscle and smart choices. Personally one can say that an alpha male has an extremely developed individual. For the most part one can say that an alpha male is an innovative person. He doesn't believe that he has to follow the crowd. There must be something distinctive about the person that inspires so many.

It is not a common trait. Artists, writers and poets typically are the types of people who have an aptitude for creativity. One is believed to be creative if she tends to do similar things to others however in a different manner. Also, the term "creativity" is thought to be used to achieve a specific result obtained through a method which is distinct from typical techniques. Creativeness is about standing above the rest of the pack. You will stand out from your competitors because you've an edge in your creative work. A male who is alpha is an entrepreneur.

People who are not creative tend to stagnate within their lives. Alpha males cannot stay at a level. It is his job to ensure that the momentum is maintained and to keep the wheels spinning. To do this, he should ensure that his group is not the same as a stagnant pool. The leader must make sure that his group runs rather than a stagnant one. Being an artist Alpha males know the methods by which it is possible to not only boost the effectiveness of the group, but also ensure maximal participation and ensure enjoyment while doing it.

Why Is Creativity So Important A Trait For An Alpha Male?

Being innovative is the key to success when it comes to cutting-edge competitiveness. There are many organizations, whether they are people or groups, who have the potential to challenge your skills at what that you boast you're a expert in. If you are the top man in the group, it puts an additional responsibility to ensure you are always ready to face a standoff. The ability to think creatively gives your group anxiety when it comes to these standoffs.

Creative people are one who is open to the vast array of possibilities. He would never be hesitant to try something that is that is different from the norm. He'd be willing to give a green light to the most innovative ideas that are a bit out of the ordinary and would inspire young minds to develop your own ideas to improve and increasing the effectiveness of the team.

Creativity indicates that the human brain is just as significant as human muscles. This means that the way you do and the way you process your thoughts are as important aspects in determining the status of your male apex as others qualities could be in your. When you're inventive, you are automatically opening your mind up to a vast number of trials and errors. When you allow yourself to make these kinds of making mistakes, you're being able to learn. Only by failing that you learn. Anyone who consistently wins is learning little.

The group is regularly competing with various other groups. It's how it's always been. From the earliest days of Earth, mankind has always been competitive. The struggle to stay alive by eliminating the other has been a part of the genes of our species. Yet, all groups are close to the same level of proficiency that other groups. Competition has grown so that there's not a lot of differences between randomly selected rivals. Technical know-how, talent and technological know-how are identical for all. What can one do to be sure to win? It's all in the imagination. A leader who is innovative enough to open the way to winning for his people is a leader. Being open to new possibilities and perspectives isn't enough. Alpha leaders must have the courage to take on whatever necessary to apply his ideas in real-world terms.

Tolerance

In a world that is so competitive, it is not one that allows you to take a break to breathe and take a breath. It's important to not only win the race but that we also do not fall apart due to the pressure it puts us to. A male who is the alpha ensures that his team survives the race, and that it doesn't fall short in completing the race.

Personally one can say that an alpha male one who is characterized by high tolerance. He's a quiet gentle, patient and composed man who is able to take all the time on earth to be attentive to the person who is least productive in the system. He will always be willing to settle at a table, have coffee with you and talk to you about your problems regardless of how hectic his work schedule is. A male who is an alpha has the capacity to handle not only the strain in managing the team, as well as the responsibility that comes with leading the group towards successful outcomes. A true alpha man doesn't snap, and rarely is found glaring at someone's an ineffective results. A leader of the Alpha group starts by calling the person not acting to him, and then gives him an enjoyable conversation and encourages the person to perform better. It is rare to see an alpha male yelling at his subordinates over minor motives. An alpha will never be able to listen to someone in the presence of his coworkers. They would prefer to make it the privacy of his own home. If it's an alpha boss who you have to deal with and you've been scolded to ear It is likely you've done an act that was really wrong or aggravated the severity of your performances. The best feature of leaders who are alpha can be that they provide you with the chance to rectify the wrongs you have committed.

A straight face, well-balanced physique with straight backs, an emoji or a face that is smiling Alpha males represent the ideal embodiment of love and patience. They're not self-centered or introverts. They can tell you where they are not right without causing offence to them. The endurance of their members is very high and you are able to count on them to navigate through calm seas.

Chapter 9: Masculinity A Changing Concept

This is the ninth and final chapter in this book. The focus will be on the changing concept of what it takes to be an individual in this chapter. Let's challenge the rigid notion of masculinity, and see whether it's able to wax or fade or it is not.

Alpha males are an absolute leader in the group. It is the man who is thought to be a man with masculine characteristics such as a strong physical appearance, endurance, and toughness. This type of masculinity are undergoing major transformations within the last couple of decades. The concept of the male who is alpha has evolved significantly over the years.

In the conventional sense of masculinity, it is not able to tolerate things as lighthearted and humorous such as comedy. But, an Alpha male should be a funny man. He's the narrator of the group, and the anecdote giver and experience-sharing. Humour is an essential part of living and is sometimes required.

To keep a group with each other, occasionally a dose of humour are a must. A male who is an alpha knows not only how to create laughs, but also make jokes for himself. He can laugh at jokes and not to take them too seriously.

A male who is an alpha can be described as an empathetic man, and not the rigid model he's believed to be. The ability to be flexible is an excellent feature in the alpha male's hat since they can adapt to changing and new circumstances and is not a stagnant person.

Flexibility is the thing that sets the Alpha males apart from normal men. Alpha males know when to bend knees and also when to take the sword. Alpha males are wise enough to be able to tell what to say and when to be quiet.

The term endurance refers to being able to sustain and survive. This trait allows you to remain even in the midst of a tough competition. It is possible that the odds are against you. Lady luck might not be on your favour and you might be struggling, however it is a good thing you be able to survive it is believed that you will endure. Alpha males have their endurance levels very high.

Tactics is a trait that the typical alpha male was lacking. In the past the alpha male could have never imagined possessing the characteristic of tact. It is the art of knowing when you should do, when to do it and the best way to influence, talk and conduct yourself in order to make the most suitable solution for you. Without tact the world would be chaos in the present. A leader knows the most effective ways to gain the best outcomes for his group.

The capacity to change is a precious trait. Your ability to change is a sign of your character and state of mind. The process of evolution isn't a matter of play for children. It requires a lot of dedication to change into a different self. It means you've let go of your past self and are now ready to accept certain changes to your lifestyle. Alpha males are always looking to grow.

It is the process of learning that keeps us motivated. It can be found anywhere in the world. There's no such thing that is'sufficient learning'. The knowledge pool is vast and nobody is able to drink it all and has lived. Alpha males are always keen to know more. The desire to know more is what drives him towards new things to be discovered and undiscovered. The student not only comes to learn about things he did not have before, but also recognizes the immenseness of everything.

In contrast to the conventional model, where an alpha male is more inclined to rule over education, but our current generation of alpha males isn't so much a closed-minded man. He is willing to learn even in the simplest of sources. As an Alpha male, it is not necessary to have the presence of a professor or a class for them to gain knowledge. For them, learning is a continuous cycle that runs through their brains.

The main message of this chapter is the perception of a typical male who is alpha is changing rapidly and with good reason, in contrast to the rigid and unwavering alpha male of the past, the current model is more realistic as well as practical and achievable.

Chapter 10: The Alpha Mindset

When you are done to work, be sure to congratulate yourself since you have finally understood the necessity of being an Alpha. At some point, all people will get bored of being beta. Not everyone is willing or has the desire to make the initial step. It's the most important quality required for an Alpha male. And you've already got it.

However, that's not the only mental changes required for success with this undertaking. Self-confidence is crucial in order to become effective in the next few months. It's also among the main traits that distinguish males who are alpha. It's unfortunate that this is the thing the majority of betas don't have. It's also a fair possibility that you've not completely built up your confidence in yourself since you do not think of yourself as an Alpha.

Enhancing your self-image above all Everything else

It is said that self-confidence can take several years to establish and just a couple of hurtful or insulting words can be destroyed. People are generally nervous and are aware of the way others perceive their appearance. That's why people want to succeed at pleasing other people or to be an example for others to be inspired by.

There are a handful of very charismatic and attractive people who seem naturally confident. The people who are these can be recognized when they're in the school. They might be handsome, attractive or simply great speakers or any combination of all these traits. In the end, they'll be more involved within their groups of friends and will continue to increase confidence in themselves with time.

The opposite, however, is applicable to those who are self-conscious and shy. Some do not have a clear understanding with their talents and talents in the beginning developmental stage of life in the social world, especially during high school. In reality, it is the time where they have to showcase their most in order to show appreciation for themselves. This means that their capacity to develop confidence in their own self is diminished, making them betas when they reach adulthood. Additionally, they tend to stay off speaking in public which means they are less likely to take on speaking engagements generally.

In the end that's the challenge for the majority of betas when they depend too heavily on their social media image to build confidence in themselves. They limit themselves, accept more opportunities, lose their actively involved in social life, and eventually have a hard time believing that they are the star they're meant become.

It is the reason you have to develop a mindset of self-motivation. You must not allow your self-image from diminishing due to the opinions of other people. Also, you must let go of the social media image you have and concentrate initially on your own image. Keep in mind that when you're an alpha person, you'll be able to have a new and fresh identity for the duration you want.

Being Self-Reliants

The next section is made up of methods that make use of the strengths as well as weaknesses to help with motivational self-talk. At present, you have be focusing on preventing you from being worried about your image on the social scene. It might seem contradictory initially, particularly since this is a book about being an Alpha. However, remember that you must have confidence to implement positive change solely for the sake respect for yourself and not to get lots of praise and boosts to your ego from the people around you. That's why you should not depend on other people to help you build your self-esteem.

for 30 days, stop you from speaking about everything to colleagues, with a particular focus on the progress that you'll be making over the remainder of the book. Surprise them towards the time the month is over by unveiling the new version of you. If you're active on social media, limit your postings and updates to just the most essential information. For the moment, you can try to keep your posts modest and observe what a pleasure you feel when doing what is right without telling others about it.

Chapter 11: The Alpha Habits

Remember that in the end others will be able to forget your mistakes and weaknesses that they've exposed to them. With sufficient time and time, they'll also overlook the positive things they know about your character. All of these qualities - - both the good and negative - will be lingering within your head. You must discover your strengths before you can create a strong identity, that which is appropriate for an Alpha.

Yes, it's difficult to boost your self-confidence, particularly if you've absconding with your own for a time time. It's not impossible if you only take a tiny step each time. First thing to accomplish is to recognize your strengths that are crucial elements of your new"alpha" brand. The strengths you have are these:

1. Talents and Skill - Each individual has their own talent and set of abilities which

they can utilize during their life. Like we said earlier that not all people get the opportunity to let their talent shine when they are young. If you're still not admiring your talent right now, then continue to dream of becoming an alpha.

2. Work and Education Academic achievements as well as job performance are proof that have your priorities in order. It is possible that you are still studying at the moment, but at the age of adulthood, these are among the best resources you could have when you are looking to become an Alpha.

3. Values Do you have a particular cause or accomplishments you can be happy about? Are you a volunteer in a non-profit group or engage in volunteering? A man who is self-confident can give back as well. Being aware of this ability now can provide you with a boost of determination.

4. Your Character: Can you recognize positive qualities that you possess? Are you a dedicated professional, a perpetual learning enthusiast, or an individual who is a person of integrity? Keep in mind that the qualities you have that you do in your life will gain your respect.

Be aware that you have the ability to utilize these strengths to boost your confidence by practicing these strengths and achieving things. When you finish this section, you'll make goals for yourself, as well as engage in other tasks during the initial week to help you get started in the right direction. One last important thing to know prior to doing this.

Handling your weak points

Even the Alphas aren't flawless. Everyone in the world is not perfect in some aspects, regardless of whether they have the ability to fix their performance or not. Certain areas are merely superficial, while others are incorporated into a lifestyle or mentality. However, whatever your weak point is it is important to acknowledge them fully and comprehending how you can make them real possibilities.

Remember that an alpha male a lifelong student an ever-evolving student. They are able to spot their flaws and turn their weaknesses into opportunities that improve their lives. In the first paragraph in this section, it was evident that you have the quality of beta by acknowledging you're an ad-hoc beta.

The areas where you could fix are:

Bad Habits - Bad behavior stem from absence of self-control and over-stress. Be aware that bad habits do not have to be restricted to bad habits including drinking or smoking. Procrastination in various forms and routine practices that could impact productivity negatively are classified as undesirable habits.

Insufficient Financial Intelligence The term "financial IQ" refers to the ability to create goals, manage the right investments, monitor your expenditures and earn income. Be aware that an ego-driven male who has a bare pocket squanders his appeal not just for his colleagues but women too.

Physical Characteristics The first thing to note is that it is possible that your physical traits can be advantages. However, there's always the possibility of improvement. The improvement of your physical attributes and well-being will form an integral component of your thirty days towards becoming an Alpha.

Being an Achiever

Be aware that only your mindset will determine the distinction between an alpha and beta, mainly due to it being crucial to be successful throughout the next chapters. The Alpha attitude is easy to grasp, but it is challenging to keep. For this to be achieved it is necessary to have an goal-oriented mindset, and constantly establish goals which will give your motivation after you have achieved the goals.

In the next 30 days, you must set goals for each day that are based on your strengths and weakness. The goal is to improve one of your strengths, or fix a weak point. This will not only assist in shaping your personal image, but it can help you get the required motivation whenever you achieve an aim. Be connected to your desires and embrace the weaknesses you have.

Be aware that you must perform this daily throughout the month to transform these actions into a habit. Also make sure you maintain your personal journal every day and keep daily entries. To keep yourself motivated, be sure you include a motivational quote in your entries about your day. The quotes can be taken from famous people in history or crafted from your personal phrases. Be aware that not everything you are able to learn through the written word could be applied to the real world more effectively. Additionally, it's amazing to share an update about something feels like something that you are able to relate to.

Chapter 12: Looking The Part

Perhaps you've embraced the mindset of alpha in your life and you're time to start looking at the complete set of. One reason for this to be done first, before health, is because you're looking to see outcomes quickly. Believe it or not being an alpha is a breeze, but it is difficult to keep for the long haul.

The Alpha Posture

It is impossible to pull off the'alpha' male' look with the right, masculine position. You'd be surprised by how it will improve how you appear, regardless of the clothes you are wearing or what your waist is. The way you stand can separate men who have a noble character from men who women will not even touch if they had the 10-foot pole. So, without further delay this is what you should keep in mind for the correct posture

Standing straight and appearing elegant and confident is among the primary objectives of having a great posture. Standing straight means you will increase the height of your body, which is essential for attracting ladies.It helps to make the appearance of being more healthy overall. In the next 30 days, you should practice on bringing your weight towards the middle part on your foot. Then, lift your chest up and keep your shoulders in a straight line and then stick your butt to the side.

The importance of sitting straight is that a majority of people find it difficult to maintain the correct posture when sitting than standing. One reason for this is that some people believe they are able to be able to get away with a bad standing posture with ease. In addition, they are spending more time in a sitting position that they appear to be unable to keep the correct posture all often time. Over the course of 30 days, you should be mindful of your posture and look you can keep it straight during your sitting. While working for extended durations, you can set an alarm each 15-30 minutes for you to keep a firm grip on your body.

Chin Up. The second aspect of the alpha posture is vital particularly when you are having conversations. It helps you appear more professional and also helps your appearance and feeling more assured. Make sure you maintain your level head and to keep eye contact while speaking. Try this for thirty days. Also, you should "practice" your posture at your home, in front of the mirror.

The Alpha Grooming

A well-groomed alpha male regardless of the time. Some say you shouldn't evaluate a book solely by the cover, yet a lot people do this nevertheless. It's not about morality. It's simply something that's true as far as morals and social customs go. If you're well-dressed then you'll get more respect than men dressed like a bunch of bums. The next 30 days, be aware of these grooming suggestions:

1. Always dress in mature Clothing Always wear mature clothing Clothing and fashion are two things that can be easily mastered for being an Alpha. First, you must always wear appropriate attire. Do not overdress or wear a t-shirt in any situation. Be mindful of the type of clothing. Beware of shirts that have profane or unprofessional designs. Instead, aim to wear simple but stylish. When you're not sure, opt to darker and neutral shades as they work for most kinds of skin.

2. It's a good idea to Trim your hair. Here's a proven truth: just a handful of males can have the head of a caveman or facial hair while looking great. The style is almost

only available to Hollywood celebrities, millionaires model and musicians. In the real world having your hair cut sleek and tidy can make you appear older and professional. One of the rules in relationships is that you should have shorter hair than females as it can look odd.

3. The stubble can be acceptable; however, full Beards aren't - in regards to facial hair, it's impossible to go wrong using stubble since it can create a masculine appearance instantly. Make sure to trim or trim it regularly to stop your stubble from becoming over the top.

4. It's nice to smell good Body sprays, gels for showers and deodorants because they have a good reason. It's because they wish to create a pleasant enjoyable experience by allowing the senses of smell, sight as well as when they meet girls, taste and touch.Smelling pleasant makes to make

you feel more comfortable and memorable for women you meet. Keep in mind that you'll never know which day you'll be meeting your next prospective client. This being said you should make it a included in your routine.

Prepping Up

Over the next seven days, it's possible to revamp your wardrobe. Buy new clothes and throw out the clothing you've been wearing in your teens. If you are shopping for clothing the most important rule is to pick the clothes you want to wear. The minimum requirement is that your choice should be made by your personal style. It should also give a impression of authenticity of your style. As you're doing this You should think about changing your cut.

Don't forget that grooming doesn't only about appearance and clothes. Grooming also involves being healthier and looking better. These will all be covered in the following chapter.

Chapter 13: Living Like The Legend

The term "alpha" does not exist solely to show off. It is essential to be strong as well as active. Also it is not a good idea to become a slouch and known as a legend. However, more important is that you need to strive for an objective. This means that you have to always consider your image of yourself into everything you perform.

However it takes time to get in shape and attain the physique of a pro. It is essential to make regular adjustments to your routine.

How to control your habits

The most effective way to take control over your health in the future is to take control of your lifestyle. The first step is to take an examination of the weak points which affect your health. At this point, you must already be aware of what you must address within your life. Are you a victim of any issues with addictions like smoking and alcoholism or pornography? These are some of the obstacles that could be harmful to your health in the longer term or in the immediate future.

However, in order to eliminate a habit completely one must develop the new behavior which will replace the old one. It should be done as a supplement to your daily goals you set from the beginning of the chapter. Below are some good habits that can help you distract your attention from bad things:

Walk No matter the person you are and what you're into and where you are there is always time to walk briskly an everyday routine. In the coming 30 days, aim to do 30 minutes or one hour of brisk, vigorous walking daily. It can be done when you return home from work, going to the store for groceries and any other time when your mind requires to have some time to rest and get back on track. This can help relieve tension and help to keep the weight off through the burning of around 300 calories during a session.

Get a Good Night's Sleep Alphas require their vitality at a high level when he is in the most need of it. It is because of its simplicity that majority of people do not realize the significance of sleeping in the correct time and obtaining the proper quantity of sleep. If you're able to last longer at parties or the bed doesn't mean that you shouldn't get sleep. The key to sleeping properly is to organize your day-to-day routine carefully. In the coming thirty days, establish an established bedtime, and then take your time sleeping when you've had a hard time getting sleep prior to bed because of unforeseen factors. One simple way to help get this done is to perform the vigorous walking exercise mentioned earlier, about an hour prior to when you plan to go to sleep.

"Take a cool shower" Cold showers offer a variety of health benefits proven to be beneficial that Alphas reap from. It helps ease anxiety, ease muscle strains and increase your energy levels, increase circulation and in tightening pores. Naturally, it's an effective way to avoid your body from smelling for the duration of the day. In the coming 30 days, make sure you get a refreshing shower each morning in order to boost your energy. Be aware that an alpha male will not shy away from any challenge. Begin the day with completing something betas are unable to manage.

Make your body weapon The body belongs to your brain as being the most valuable resource you'll ever own throughout your life. The men who have the most are not using excuses like a inability to find the time or genetics in order to take the control of their appearance. It isn't necessary to join a gym in order to shape up. In the coming 30 days, do pushups and sit ups and squats daily for the most amount you can, however, you should not do less than 50 reps each. In normal practice, you'll divide the number of sets into several. These exercises can be done however you like.

Take care of your Skin. In the same way that you stay in shape by taking treatment of your skin can give you a feeling of confidence and beautiful. Be sure to use an appropriate facial cleanser made for men. If not, you can try gentle products especially if you suffer from acne such as shaving cuts or pimples. Over the next thirty days, create your daily skin care routine that starts by washing your face twice every daily.

Be mindful of the food you consume Apart from drinking alcohol, it is important to be aware of the foods you eat. In the coming 30 days, stay away from the foods high in sugar, salt as well as trans-fats. The next chapter will provide a step-by-step guidance on how to create your own routine for eating every day within the next section.

Stopping your bad habits

Willpower and self-control are essential in order to keep the bad habits you have cultivated under your control. It's not easy, bad habits are easier to establish, but they can be difficult to break. The reason is that the human brain is programmed to focus on immediate gratification that is evoked by primitive responses. However the long-term benefits usually demand an element of sacrifice, like time as well as money and work before they can be experienced.

Concentrating on the longer-term impact of your decisions requires an intervention from your higher thought or more rational thoughts.And staying focused and rational is what the alphas excel in. In the coming 30 days, make it a point to consistently make the right choice and plan what you will reward yourself for having done so.

An easy way to ensure you to break those bad habits is to give yourself the option of either doing the wrong thing instead, or to follow one of the list of healthy behaviors found in the Chapter. It is also possible to engage in different productive tasks that are based on the chapter 2 The Alpha Habits in the section "Being an Achiever".

Chapter 14: Living The Alpha Life

After you've adopted the style, mindset and good habits that are typical of an alpha male it's time to begin making those more significant lifestyle modifications which you must follow daily. These are the habits and practices that will bring the best results and enhance your quality of life over time. These include a couple of practices in finance that betas typically aren't able to adjust to.

Take Charge of Your life

A male who is an alpha must always take on the role of leader. The key to charisma is how well he can recognize the importance of respect and confidence. This is a benefit for all occasions. This may seem easy however it is hard to learn.

You can always manage one step at an time. This time you are able to begin making a difference in your daily life by following three simple steps:

1. Being a good listener A leader can recognize the best in others and inspires people to make use of this. It is essential when it comes to your career as well as in your school, work, or business. Being a judge of your own will affect your character which makes you a liked person all around. Over the next thirty days, try to establish trust with your coworkers by finding their strengths and encourage them to make use of them.

2. Being financially sound A man who is financially sound knows how to manage cash. A different rule to follow in relationships is to make sure you pay for meals. Therefore, you must ensure that you have money saved up to cover a rainy day. Over the next 30 days, you should save minimum $10 per day through cutting costs or searching for

opportunities for an more revenue. Additionally, you should invest your expertise in the area of investments.

3. Being a gentleman - While Alpha males are at times intimidating, they should remain jovial and gracious, not just to women, however, to men also. The qualities of a gentleman are used in all your daily actions in your the world. It's all it takes is a small amount of compassion and being humble.For instance, being apologetic or admitting to your faults is not a sign of weakness. It's actually opposite. In the coming 30 days, be courteous to those in your vicinity and notice how grateful they are to you.

Eating Right

It's no surprise that Alpha males have an appropriate weight. It's more than eating three meals daily. The key is to eat in accordance with what you are trying to accomplish. In simple terms, if you are looking to shed pounds, you require a caloric deficit that can be accomplished by eating less calories than what your body requires. If you're thin who is in the need of more weight, then you'll require caloric surplus, which is the reverse of a deficit in caloric. Both are essential elements of any diet, and are measured by measuring your daily calories by using calculators like these:

Calorie King - www.calorieking.com

Free Dieting -www.freedieting.com

A Calorie Counter - www.acaloriecounter.com

In the coming 30 days, you must decide if you're in need of an excess or a deficit in calories and set a goal for a decrease between 500 and 1000 calories in your food choices. Simply check food labels or search online databases to find the calorific value of certain products. It is best using Calorie Counter by My Fitness Pal on Android gadgets. Otherwise, use online sites like www.caloriecount.com or www.myfitnesspal.com.

Be aware that the purpose behind diets is to limit the amount of food you consume and not the frequency at which you eat. To help keep the hunger at bay, you could try dividing your calories throughout the day into 4 portions throughout the day. This will allow you to full of hunger all entire day.

Beating fears

Every person on the entire world has a fear of some thing. The difference between an alpha beta is that the former know how to face their fears using a method that is effective. It is possible to view fears as weaknesses, or an opportunity to make room for improvement. In the next 30 days, you should do something is something you're typically afraid of doing. Naturally, it must be productive or a creative endeavor that you are afraid of, such as being in public, of rejection, etc. - and not anything trivial, like fear of spiders or heights etc.

It doesn't matter whether there's an opportunity to grow your company, contacting a woman who you're interested in or entering into a contest which you've never thought of participating in. A man who is an alpha takes the opportunities to not only gain, but to enhance his life in the process.

This may sound like cheesy however, believing you're an alpha male, and taking on your fear head-on can boost confidence. In the case of example, if have a fear of speaking to people set a goal to take part in public speaking and test how confident you feel with confidence that you have gained.

Chapter 15: Who Is An Alpha Male?

Alpha male is the definition used to define an Alpha

Alpha males are the most assertive, dominating, and usually successful type of male. He is able to follow his own way even when it's contrary to the norm or belief of society.

He has a strong drive to influence his surroundings instead of being shaped by the environment around him.

He has the ability to safeguard himself and the people around him. He is able to lead others, and is able to socially share his mission without degrading the personal beliefs or values of the others.

He's direct and clear about his goals, motives and requirements to all and especially the other sexual sex. He doesn't accept less than wants.

Alpha males take the responsibility for his actions, and is not apologizing to others or his circumstances for the mistakes he makes. He doesn't get overcome by emotions and believes only in the presence of evidence that supports his beliefs.

He is adored and appreciated by everyone. He exudes a swagger and charm Women are drawn by his charm and charisma. He's sociable, and an enthralling person to be around.

What is Being Alpha NOT about!

Alpha males aren't a sexist jerk who is often mistaken for. Certain kinds of men feel they are more popular by putting other individuals down. They tend to be irrational and are able to pick fights on any topic.

These characteristics are not a description of the Alpha male.

Men of these kinds typically feel insecure, yet they try to conceal their vulnerability by presenting as tough. They're usually arrogant and mistakenly believe they are confident.

The males in these categories are influenced by others, and they typically prefer to be at the center of things so that they can be noticed. Certain people are willing to accept their machinations, with the exception of men who are the alpha.

Application Exercise

1. Definition of an Alpha Male in your own terms.

2. List the characteristics the ideal male alpha should have.

Chapter 16: The Qualities Of An Alpha Male

The Attitude of the Alpha

One of the most important characteristics that defines an alpha male is that he is genuinely concerned little about what people consider him or about the way he behaves. The alpha male rarely thinks of the way he's perceived by other people.

The masculine alpha man has instilled within him all the characteristics of masculinity: dedication, determination, passion on the task at hand, determination, charm style, charisma, etc.

The man who's the most dominant puts forth any effort necessary in order to be the most effective possible person that he can be. He will not settle for anything the lesser of what he is entitled to and he isn't content with the previous accomplishments. He constantly pushes himself out of his comfort area and is willing to explore the unknown in the event that he's sure that it's the correct path for what he wants.

The reason women love males who are Males attractive?

Alpha males don't constantly praise women or appeal their self-esteem. They do not care about winning the attention of women since they do not care about getting it back.

Although the male of Alpha is awed by women's sexual chemistry but he'd rather avoid it rather than accept unwelcome, manipulative and disrespectful sexual behavior of women.

This attitude of an alpha male can make women seem unnaturally drawn to him.

Males who are Alpha males naturally interact and typically maintain conversations that are interesting, fascinating and enjoyable when they are with women.

The majority of Alpha males have an innate sense of humor and their wit. They truly enjoy with women in both ways sexually and not. They'll also keep at least a few casual friendships with females.

Alpha Males are Sociable People

Females love alpha males for their leadership qualities and drive, passion goals-driven personality, their confidence in independence as well as their confidence levels.

Application Exercise

1. What characteristics of the Alpha male are you lacking?

2. Note down the steps you need to take for you to develop your Alpha masculine qualities that you are lacking.

Chapter 17: How We Lost Our Alpha Status!

You Were Born As an Alpha

Your genes were encapsulated with the qualities of an alpha, and were designed to be bold courageous, confident and courageous.

Take note of a child and their childlike traits like determination, passion and zeal. You are able to name it. They are qualities that you're expected to improve by as you grew older as you learned and gained the experience.

The environmental and social constraints have suppressed these traits. So, now you're expected to behave in a specific manner to conform to society's norms.

How Our Environment Changed Us

As time the attributes of these traits became lost and lifestyle was accepted.

When we were children it was impossible to control what we could change about the choices of the environment or manner of raising your children.

When we were youngsters, we were all blessed with older adults as mentors we admired And even as children we modeled all traits of our earlier teachers.

The majority of children were bullied throughout their primary and secondary schools. This also influences their outlook on life. They think they're the being a victim, and are raised to be apathetic and incapable of having the courage to speak to defend them.

In addition, when we did not succeed or erred We were ridiculed as well as beaten and mocked. These actions taught us to think that mistakes are naive, and it was not acceptable to fail.

Over time for us to stay on the perfectionism that we have our team never tried something new, and instead clung to the things we had observed worked for other people, but we never tried the new ideas to see if they work for us.

What causes some men to become Beta Males.

Our mentors were our first lens through which we viewed the world. A large portion aspects of our early perception of the world is still present to this day. Therefore, if we had teachers who were like the beta group, we clone every aspect of their personality.

We were raised to seek approval from all but us. Our parents would seek approval from our parents first, later, from our relatives and friends and finally to our schools, and finally our wives and finally our employers at work.

Make it clear that I don't mean that anyone is disrespected, as you're trying to show that you don't need their approval. Never! !

If you do find yourself engaging in behavior that you realize is clearly incorrect or clearly against the things you want, simply to please others is where the issue comes in.

Additionally, the majority of people had motherly and nurturing mothers who were beautiful and kind, yet on the flip opposite, were dominant and controlling. It's a paradox which has taught people to fear women and to desperately attempt to please women so that we can gain their satisfaction.

Chapter 18: The Beta Male

Definition of a Beta Male

Beta male Beta male character is mean typical, moderate, risk averse male. The Beta male lacks confidence, charisma as well as masculinity, which is generally is associated with the winners.

The male of the beta group tends to be shy, intelligent calm and quiet. The typical stereotype of him is a geek or as a good male. He's submissive, dependent on women since the belief is that she will reciprocate with admiration.

He also tends to optimistically expect positive results and the desired outcomes, rather than firmly taking actions in order to get them.

The Mentality of the Beta Male

The male who is beta usually has an inflated self-esteem based on factors such as intelligence, attractive looks and family status however, they lack confidence to enhance these qualities.

People usually seek out every opportunity to boast about their achievements, status as well as wealth and possessions to impress the people around them and also the women they want to impress.

Beta males typically possess a normal-looking physique they lack confidence, and have poor social abilities. Most of the time, they will use their words to impress or impress women. They may also be timid and not able to engage with women.

Beta Males are Approval Seekers

Beta males are emotional insecure as he obtains his confidence from the approval from others. He is extremely upset when people critique him and speak negatively about him.

Anything is possible to ensure that his followers always appreciate his character. He usually goes out of his way to please others and hopes that they will treat him nicely in return.

The people who give their all in support of are not ready to even move one inch to accommodate them.

Beta Males Are Non-Confrontational

The Beta Male allows individuals to talk about them and treat him in the most disrespectful, condescending way. He lacks the grit to speak up.

They let women be the leader in their relationship and to make the most important choices. The male betas generally permit women to be disrespectful or walk around them since they don't wish to cause women to feel uncomfortable.

How Beta Males Treat Women

Beta males are male that is typically tagged as nice by females. He thinks that putting cash on women and performing favors for their benefit is a most effective way to attract women and retain her attention.

Beta males are inclined to put women as well as other individuals in a pedestal. The male betas love women for everything regardless of whether they breathe in, and also exhale. They will agree with anything she says or opinions she has.

They're always financially affluent and are generally always at their fingertips. Beta males actually are worshippers of the ground that women are walking upon.

This attitude is maintained until the point that they turn into dissatisfied and angry womanizer.

Mistakes Beta Males Make With Women

Beta males is willing to do anything for women's affection if they feel that he has a chance of finding a gorgeous partner for a long time or a future spouse. They will go on for many hours, days, weeks or even days enticing ladies, and offering financial favors as well as financial assistance.

Most of the time, beta males let themselves become female's male friend. They let them be angry, whine, and complain about other men who leave them feeling depressed angry, irritated, or devastated.

The phenomenon persists for quite a lengthy time throughout the lives of males in the beta group, but they start to see that the opportunities they have to spend time in love with women romantically as well as sexually is a challenge.

It is the time when the beta male shifts their attitude of being a devoted fan of women, to becoming the harsh critic and demonizer of women. This paradigm shift is also a change from a mindset of profound admiration, reverence and love of women, to anger with, bitterness and anger towards women.

Beta Males Sexual Strategy

Beta Males are aware that their sole chance to have a female companionship probably come from women who are prostitutes or run girls. They invest to spend so much time with never allow their bodies to be touched and, in the meantime, these they could also be offering other males the sex they want. Only orgasms are triggered by the act of masturbation.

The males who have gone affected by this experience are driven by an urge to take egotistical emotional revenge against women. They transform into rapists physically and emotionally abusive of women. Additionally, they may date and rape women and drug addicts in order so that they can profit.

Application Exercise

1. What traits that are characteristic of the male beta you observe yourself to exhibit?

2. Make a list of actions to alter these beliefs.

Chapter 19: Signs That You're A Beta Male

You Don't Feel Like Your Life Is Getting Better

If you're feeling like you're not passionate about the work, life or activity, then that you're a male beta. It's likely that you've given up on the goals you set, and see every aspect of life as an obligation and you look at the weekends as a way to relax, because it's the only time for you to detach yourself from the reality of your life.

You Never Face Your Bully

The bullies take it upon those they believe as weak, because they aren't sure how to solve the issues they face rather than take it out on others. The weak are their easiest to target. If you notice yourself getting taken in by other people this could be a sign that you're a beta.

Rely On Others to Make Decision for You

It's a sign that you're a beta man if individuals make your decisions. There's a distinct difference the time when someone suggests things to you, and when they transform their lives to the ones you live. It's like living with the realities of others but not living in your own life. You are in the deepest part of yourself it is clear that this isn't the way you would like to live, but you do it anyway in order to win their trust.

You are Physically Weak

Physical weakness is usually linked with illness or insecurity. Males are generally not motivated to have a great physique. They tend to play video games or computer games to cost to their health. They will target you in case you seem weak.

You're In the Friendzone

If you're friendly with women and provide favors or provide financial aid to ensure to reciprocate their favors by having a sex date, you're already part of the circle. The result is that you'll be attracting women who are only interested in favors on your finances, but without a sexual attraction to the relationship with you.

It's a matter of ability and confidence to maintain the flame of attraction.

You Can't Say No and Stand Your Ground

If you're unable to voice your views and express about your thoughts without fear of getting onto people's feet, then it's likely that you're a beta.

If you aren't able to be adamant, other people tend to take advantage of your flaws in being a pleasing person. It will lead you to the position of not being appreciated, and you're unhappy. Don't be a victim of others. and say yes to yourself.

There is no way to assist others in the first place without first helping yourself.

People Make Fun of You

Bring value to those surrounding you to ensure you get treated with respect. You will be criticized by others and mock them if they think you're the one who is the weak link within the team.

Your life revolves Around Past Times

If you're taking in too many shows as well as playing too many games or taking up all of your time surfing the web It's likely that you're an adolescent. The forms of entertainment you choose to watch are good for you if used properly. You do it in order to keep yourself from performing a task or because you're lazy.

Reduce your time spent watching TV as well as channeling the time into more productive tasks. There are endless possibilities that are hidden within your. They're not fully realized because you are addicted to media to divert yourself from real life.

You Make Excuses

If you're caught in the cycle of justifying your mistakes then you're likely to be being a beta. If you don't meet the obligations you've said you would do, it's making yourself look bad. There are many excuses you can come up with, but your main reason for refusing to take action is because you're afraid to fail or simply do not want to. This makes it difficult for you to cope with the world as it is.

You Lack Style

Beta males aren't too concerned about how they look. They do not wear clean or well-fitting clothes and appear to be dressed as if they're out of style. There is no need to buy expensive clothes. It's about styling and grooming. There is no cost to dress well these days.

Application Exercise

1. What traits of a beta male traits do you see you to be displaying?

2. Make a list of actions to alter these beliefs.

Chapter 20: Anyone Can Become An Alpha Male

Change the environment around you to change your Situation

The majority of males were raised within an environment that helped them develop traits of a beta male. If you want to change your status, changing your surroundings.

The intense social and environmental influences made males reluctant to take on new challenges in anxiety of failing. They wait for things to be taken care of by them, instead of acting, never being in a position to confront the bullying they faced in their the early years of their lives.

Males are the majority to carry these characteristics in their early years, all the way to teenagers, even into the age of adulthood.

Being Beta is Feminine, Not Masculine.

Beta males aren't good.

Being a beta is directly linked with being feminine. Beta males are typically female in their attitude. They are the reason women adore these guys as friends.

The majority of men find females attractive even though some attributes of beta are associated with being feminine. Women don't necessarily consider men who are feminine attractive. they only like males who exhibit masculinity.

The majority of men can still be a good team despite these traits. The luck seems to show up upon them every once in a when they are living an existence with these traits.

Are you satisfied with your life and aren't looking for more in life? Do you prefer to wait for luck to come your way, instead of being prepared to seize opportunities? This book is very little help for you.

You are more than you think! You can be Alpha!

If you're looking to become at the helm of things you experience in your daily life, this book is going to expose your brain to fresh possibilities, as well as help your journey to become an Alpha male.

If you're looking to lure gorgeous women into your life, first you have to develop your character to match the level of a male who women find attractive.

Compensation

Compensation refers to the process by which an individual male who is who is undergoing the transition from beta status into Alpha status acts in a way that is excessive as a way to rectify past failures and mistakes.

Transformation into Alpha males will take time to fully implement.

You won't be able to get it right at the very beginning.

The lion, The animal kingdom's Alpha typically stays at a distance until there's an urgent need to protect his family or defend his property and he is ready to take on his task.

There is no need to conduct yourself in a manner to draw the attention of others who notice that has transformed. Change is natural with regular work.

This could result in a reverse impact of presenting as someone weak, who puts in a smug appearance of strength to cover up his fears.

You'll be noticed by others by the actions they use to control you don't are effective.

The eminent alpha is a person who has all the traits already in his body and does not try to display his "awesome" personality.

Chapter 21: The Mentality Of An Alpha Male

The process of establishing an alpha male status is more about the mindset and beliefs of the Alpha male, the mentality of an alpha male. The mindset of an alpha male is the result of our mindset and mental state.

Our mindset constantly regulates our actions. The intention and the execution must coincide for behavior for it to be successful.

The concept of alpha is more an internal more than a external phenomenon. There are however, crucial external factors that make you the Alpha male.

The mindset and beliefs of an alpha male are what differentiates him from other males.

Purpose

Alpha males are man with a purpose. He has a clear idea of where he's taking his the world. He doesn't go in the direction of others in the event that it is not his choice. He creates a plan that he has set for himself, and follows it until the very end.

He's not at all influenced by what others say since he doesn't care to please others.

The women who like him are attracted by his attractiveness due to their natural attraction to men who are determined and clear. They like a man who stands out in the crowd, and who is prepared to take on any challenge to fulfill their goals.

The alpha male is courageously moving towards his vision. He is not scared of failing as failure, even though not expected of him, will not stop him from moving closer to the vision he has.

What's the purpose behind you? Did you find it? Did you record it?

Does it have a specificity? Does it have a measurement? Is it Achievable? Are you able to achieve it? Does it have a time component?

The pursuit of a goal in life and a reason for living is one of the main factors that differentiate in an alpha male from other male types.

Males are a part of reality, which is reflected in the surroundings and the social system. However, the Alpha male is the one who creates his own reality regardless of whether it differs to the world of others.

Passion

It is an energizing force which is an amalgamation of feelings - the love of and hatred. Passion is what we want to be and things that we do not want to change. The combination of these feelings is the reason behind our choices.

A male who is an alpha will be passionate about everything that he gets up to. He is not content to be mediocre and be a part of the group.

The entire tenth of their body into the work they accomplish. They're never bored. They're full of energy and passion in all they do. This can be seen in the outcomes that they generate. They always rank at the best in whatever they accomplish. They are committed to their work and never let down by situations that come their way.

The women who are passionate and have determination to be very attractive. They naturally attract guys who are passionate since they are awe-inspiring in all they accomplish. They always associate themselves with perfection.

What is it that you are passionate about? What are you able to do to fill your time that you enjoy doing, regardless of regardless if you earn profit from it or otherwise? What do you are passionate about that gives satisfaction and enjoyment?

Find three things that you are interested in.

An activity that can earn your money.

An activity that keeps you fit.

An activity that makes your mind creative.

Passion sets an alpha man apart from the rest of males. It's the reason he's driven driving him to do something instead of having a monotonous routine and routine life without enthusiasm.

Learning

A man who is an alpha commits to learning. He knows the best way to be present in today's fast-paced, ever-changing world is by acquiring something new.

The current generation is the most rapid altering generation thanks to the latest technology that is utilized in all spheres of life. This revolutionary shift that takes place every week in this generation may take years, or even decades for previous generations.

Alpha males realize that learning can as well be a process of removing wrong habits and relearning practices from the past. He does not let schooling hinder his education.

The alpha male likes to learn a bit about all things, but the alpha male is extremely proficient at one of abilities. Essential education that we require to live a fulfilling life, which is emotional intelligence, financial aptitude, interpersonal and so on. These aren't taught at school.

So an alpha male can learn outside of the boundaries of his discipline and this makes him superior to 90% of the people who don't have books. He is deemed to be culturally knowledgeable and assured.

Females are able to find an individual with this trait to be exciting and enjoyable to spend time with. They have a blast with him since there is no dull moment for him. The man is culturally educated and smart. He is also wise and is always in the lead of his peers since the man is dedicated to spending his time in advancing his own performance. Women recognize on a subconscious degree that these men have the qualities to be successful and live happily.

Do you have time to spend time studying? Do you enjoy educational TV programmes? Do you go to sessions to understand the subject? Do you enjoy educational audio recordings on your the subject of personal development? The last time you've have a book that wasn't related to your field of study?

Do you realize that when you completed three readings on the same subject that you become an expert in the area and makes you stand out from 97% of the people who don't have a reading habit?

A male who is an alpha constant student who is constantly learning how to stay relevant in a constantly changing, fast-paced world. He is constantly learning, growing as well as he's always evolving. The fact that he reads books enhances the capacity of his mind and that the information he acquires through the correct actions puts him ahead of the rest.

Leadership

Alpha males are committed to be an effective leader. They are valued and admired since they're independent and self-reliant. Alpha males are accountable to themselves unlike other types of males who have to answer to each individual except themselves.

Women are naturally drawn to the leaders since leadership is a key ingredient to the success of the world. Women seek out a man who can control his life, and is living in the present. They rely on masculine alphas who have leadership skills and "lead-her-ship".

What are your plans to assume leadership roles? What are the times you have volunteered for when you are required to fulfill the responsibilities? How often have you volunteered for a position due to the goals you've got for your job?

Although some people are against the responsibility of leading The alpha male accepts these responsibilities knowing that being a leader will greatly improve the status of an Alpha male.

When you get the chance to guide others, take the lead and claim the responsibility. You may not previously have taken on this task. But, it'll make you think outside your comfort zone, and help you to develop.

Confidence

The word confidence means that you believe in you and the capabilities of your. Alpha males are self-assured male who can make unimaginable decisions, if he believes that it is the right choice for his needs.

Confidence does not mean making perfect decisions. You must trust your gut instincts. Even when the choice turns out to be incorrect You'll be able to find a method to turn your loss into victory by learning from it.

The self-confidence of an alpha male is reflected in all areas of his existence and provides him an edge on the competition in everything that he undertakes.

Confidence is among the most attractive traits that an alpha male has. The fact that it is a trait that's noticed by women because they are drawn to confident men. They're willing to take on things that help them become better or more effective, which earn them more money.

What was the most recent time you took on something different? How often do you take the risk to pursue the activities you are passionate about?

In order to increase your confidence, first it is essential to remove negative individuals out of your life who do not recognize the potential in problems. Find friends who have a positive outlook and are cheerful find the positive within every issue. Second, it is important to develop your skills, as confidence stems from the information you have learned.

Assertiveness

The word "assertiveness" means that you display confidence or a bold, confident personality. It is the line between being passive and assertive. It's the act of handling an event in a calm and controlled way.

The alpha male might not be admired for the traits he displays, but it's sure to make the people who are his fans respect him more. The alpha male doesn't try to pretend to be who he's not just to please people.

A male who is an alpha gives immediate feedback to everything he interacts with. He isn't afraid to speak the truth, because he would like his followers to love his character. The trait of assertiveness assists him in eliminating off fakes from his world.

He is convinced that what is unique about him, and isn't going to be anything more than that to earn acceptance from people. He is aware of his shortcomings Accepts them, accepts them, and is working on them, and grows into an improved version of himself each day.

He is aware of his place on his own journey as well as the steps he'll need to follow to reach them. He's neither tentative nor is he a shapeshifter. He's real and has his real-world perspective.

The assertiveness and confidence of an alpha male can make women appreciate his style. He does not tolerate snarky remarks from women, and then immediately smacks them to their feet. He does not feel the need to put women in a position of power or to worship women. The women, however, tend to be attracted by males who don't take bullshit from them. They usually appreciate their opinions.

Although the male who is alpha tends to be confident, males who remain passive and allow life to take place. They're often not happy with everything that goes on within their own world, but they are able to let themselves become victims of the situation they're going through.

People usually complain at how poorly someone took care of them or the dire situations that await them, but don't take action to tackle these problems.

If you are able to assert yourself, regardless of making the smallest decision It gives you confidence to assert your self in larger situations. Be sure to stand to defend yourself even for simple things, even if you think they are to be insignificant. This will help you gain confidence to stand up and take on even bigger problems.

Identity

It is this attitude that distinguishes a person from others of his peers. Alpha males know that the Alpha persona is what sets him apart from all other types of males, which is why they display his Alpha identity.

Alpha males love their image as the Alpha male, which is why the alpha male doesn't attempt to fit in with social norms or social expectations in order to stand apart. It is his uniqueness that is easily recognized by the crowd.

Your identity? What differentiates you from others? What is it about you which makes you instantly recognizable by others?

The women who see his distinctness attract his unique quality he exhibits. He doesn't try to be unique since he is trying to attract women as well as individuals in his vicinity. He's different due to the fact that the way he is a person which sets him apart from other.

Goal-Driven

Goals are statements that is written to attain an ideal state or achievement at any moment in time. A male who is alpha is a set-up person with goals which he utilizes to gauge the progress he has made towards achieving the ultimate goal. The alpha male sets routine objectives that could be a weekly, daily and monthly, or some other metrics that are time bound to bring him towards achieving the goals he has set for himself.

He moves with vigor towards his objectives. He does not see any obstacle with every chance of reaching his objectives; rather there is a chance when there is a snag between him and the goals. He does not wait for ideal circumstances to accomplish his goals He is able to move forward despite conditions that surround him.

The alpha male, as everyone else, is often afraid, however, he manages the fear in a different way. He recognizes that fear may hinder him from taking actions, and thereby not achieve his objectives.

But, he is aware that fear is an illusion emotion that can be paralyzing and is an emotion that is worth compromising on or letting go of the goal. Therefore, he moves forward even though he is scared, but determinedly in the direction towards his goal.

What do you consider your weekly, daily or month-long objectives? Have you written them down? Do you have a plan to achieve these goals?

Imagine what you'd like to be three years. Record them on paper. Take note of the everyday actions you could take to bring you closer to who you'd like to be in the near future. Revise them frequently to be certain you're moving toward getting there.

Sociable

A person who is sociable who is extroverted and socially open to the those around him. He is able to initiate and hold conversations with people from any social class. Alpha males are a social person who is very enjoyable to hang out with.

He's easy-going simple, down-to-earth and jovial. He isn't one to take things to heart. He is capable of helping everyone around him feel confident and happy.

The males who are Alpha typically possess a swaying personality that allows them to mix with individuals of various kinds of personalities effortlessly. They may be loud open, honest, and provocative and smack those that are more open or free of inhibitions.

However the person could appear to be traditional gentle, courteous, cautious, and thoughtful in their way of expression when conversing with someone less conservative and more reserved.

What are the most frequent times you get to make new acquaintances and eventually make friends with the people you meet? Are you surrounded by people who enjoy your company and engage you in conversation?

You can expand your social circle to be the one one to start a conversation, and making everybody feel at ease with you.

When you do this you are choosing your own friends but not always chosen to be your friend. You should look for ways that you can be more impactful on your peers than be affected.